T0102655

CANOE CREEK B.C.

DON LOGAN

Order this book online at www.trafford.com
or email orders@trafford.com

Most Trafford titles are also available at major online book retailers.

© Copyright 2011 Don Logan.
All rights reserved. No part of this publication may be reproduced, stored in a retrieval
system, or transmitted, in any form or by any means, electronic, mechanical, photocopying,
recording, or otherwise, without the written prior permission of the author.

Printed in the United States of America.

ISBN: 978-1-4269-5875-5 (sc)

Trafford rev. 02/26/2011

 www.trafford.com

North America & international
toll-free: 1 888 232 4444 (USA & Canada)
phone: 250 383 6864 ♦ fax: 812 355 4082

INTRODUCTION

Geographically, Canoe Creek is located between the two settlement districts of Big Bar and Dog Creek on the old River Trail. My first two efforts in compiling information and photographs on this part of our Cariboo were based on these two areas. It seems that it was only a natural progression to follow up with something on Canoe Creek.

Between these small centers and outlying areas there is an overlap of the early families and individuals and I have included some never before published photos and information from these surrounding areas.

I am always amazed at the number of descendants that have delved into their family history and preserved the old photographs.

Special recognition must be given to Nancy Camille for her interest and information. Audrey Higbee, great granddaughter of old Philip Grinder, for her superb researches on the Grinder, Vedan and Hannon families. Beaunie Mumford, daughter of Lincoln Hannon and granddaughter of Old Philip Grinder, for sharing her mothers' early photographs of the "B.C. Cattle Company". Shirley Robins, for her family's photographs. Wendy Morton, great great granddaughter of Raphael Valenzuela, for her family histories, and her mother, Hazel's memories. Mildred Kalalest, for her efforts and interest in the Canoe Creek history. Darlene Louie, for preserving so many old photos. Betz Ratch, the indispensable, for doing research at the B.C. Archives in Victoria for me. Many thanks to all!

Again, last but not least, thanks to my most supportive enthusiast, Karen.

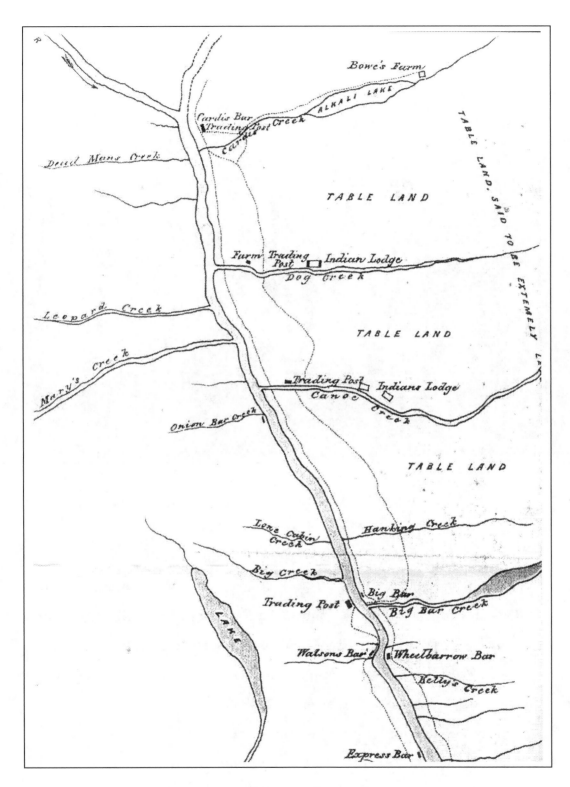

Rough Sketch of the Cayoosh District.
Drawn by Lance Corporal J. Conroy, Royal Engineer.
July 2nd 1861.

Meeting of the Central Fraser River Band Chiefs.
New Westminster 1868.
Standing: Tao Task (Canoe Creek), William, (William's Lake)
Seated: Nariah (Dog Creek), Quib Quarsla, (Alkali Lake), Se Askut
(Shushwap), Timpt Khan, (Babine Lake), Sikosalish, (Lillooet). Kam
Cosatlze,(Soda Creek), Sosastumpt, (Bridge Creek).

New Westminster was the capital of British Columbia, a site selected by
Colonel Moody of the Royal Engineers in 1859, but moved to Victoria in 1868.
The home on the right of the photo was that of Captain William Irving, his
family settled there in 1865. More about the Irving family later as son John was
one of the original investors in the British Columbia Cattle Company. The
"Irving Home" is now a museum.

THE NAME

First Nation people called it "STSWECEM'C" meaning " The place where the creek passes through".

The British Columbia Geographical Name dept. adopted officially the Name "Canoe Creek" on August 5th, 1954. Based on notes of B.C.'s Chief Geographer with reference to Simon Fraser's Journal of 1807 *"where the village here "Le Canot" and the stream "La Riviere du Canot".*

In a "Stswecem'c Xgat'tem" newsletter published in June of 2007, Harold Harry reported the following article:

Name of tribe- The Indians to be described in this paper are called "Shushwap" by the whites. The employees of the Northwest Company, who first visited them from the north, generally called them "Atnas" which is a word of Carrier derivation. They were also called "Atnah or Carrier Indians by Sir Alexander McKenzie in 1793 and by Simon Fraser in 1808. The former was probably the first white man to meet any of them, and the latter was the first white man to explore the northern and western parts of their country. This visit is remembered by a very old man, Setse'l by name, who was born in the village of Peq on Riske Creek and

Simon Fraser, explorer and partner with the Northwest Company.

was still living at Alkali Lake in 1900. He was a small boy when Simon Fraser's party came down the Fraser River with canoes. Xlo'sem, the Soda Creek chief, accompanied the party as a guide and interpreted for them. Kolpapatci'nexen 3 was at that time the chief of the Canoe Creek Band and Haxkwe'st was a noted war chief and wealthy man. He had three wives and was tall, and wore only a breechclout, excepting in the wintertime. Some of the Soda Creek Indians were the only Shushwap who had seen white men prior to Fraser's party. In many places the people thought the strangers were transformers, mythological beings, or cannibals, and consequently were very distrustful of them. Fraser gave presents of tobacco, beads and knives, to almost all the Indians he met…."

James Teit, 1864-1922.

The above quotation is from " The Shushwap"- volume 2, written by James Teit in 1909. Anthropologist Franz Boaz hired Teit, a Scotsman from the Shetland Isles, to accompany the Jesop Expedition in 1897. The goal of the expedition was to collect artifacts and information on behalf of the American Museum of Natural History. Teit was familiar with and had traveled the area on hunting and exploring trips as early as 1887. He continued his extensive travels of the interior; accumulating and documenting the history of the indigenous people after the expedition was completed.

Teit had acquired first hand information from personal interviews with knowledgeable living elders. Of note pertaining to the Canoe Creek band was the Tcexwe'pkamux "people of the pillar hollow" who wintered in the Empire Valley. Teit described their history:

"A number of this band did not use underground houses, but wintered in tents. They were greatly reduced in numbers by a war party of Lillooet who, about 1825, massacred a large camp of them wintering at the Red Butte, near Empire Valley and again by small pox in 1862. The remnants of them settled with the Canoe Creek band. This band was closely related to the Canoe creek people."…

"Small-pox epidemics have been the prime cause of this decrease. This disease has visited portions of the tribe twice, in 1862 and 1863 it was especially severe, wiping out whole villages… other bands living on the west side of the Fraser River, contracted the disease from the Chilcotin and were practically exterminated…."

Teit estimated the populations of the Empire Valley and Canoe Creek bands to be approximately 100 and 250 respectively for the year 1850, with a notation that the Empire band may have been as high as 250 to 300 as early as 1810 or 1820, before the massacre.

At the time of his writing, according to the returns of the Indian Dept., the population of the Canoe Creek band was 1903, 161 and for 1906, 163, fairly static.

The Reserve

Above is the sight that greeted Harry Marriott, on his arrival, in the early summer of 1912. He described it: *"We drove along the road again to the Canoe Creek House. A mile or so this side of the ranch house we passed through the Canoe Creek Indian Reserve in which the cabins and barns were all made of logs. A lot of them seemed to be in very poor shape, but they had a white painted church with a cross gleaming on the top of it and a large bell hanging in the bell tower on top of the church."*

Britain established Vancouver Island, as a colony, in 1849. The Hudson's Bay Company was granted proprietorial rights for ten years and in 1851 the Chief Factor, James Douglas, was appointed as Governor. In 1858 he was also appointed Governor of the new mainland Colony of British Columbia.

Prior to this time the indigenous people of the interior had virtually no interference with their life style from outsiders. The traditional Secwepemc (Shuswap) way of life was based on a seasonal relocation that revolved around hunting, gathering, and salmon fishing. They traveled and moved camp following the food supplies, returning to their winter lodges at their permanent villages. Remaining on friendly terms with their neighboring tribes was the only criteria that was needed for free travel, there had been no previous recognition of private property.

This photo was from Mary Palmantier's album marked: "Many of the homes are dirt covered on the roofs"

This more or less isolation was soon to be shattered with the influx of gold miners in 1858. As Governor of the new Colony, one of Douglas's first instructions was to reserve Indian villages and lands. This instruction was followed on January 4th 1860 with Proclamation #15, a pre-emption policy, which allowed for the acquisition of unoccupied, unreserved, and unsurveyed Crown Land in British Columbia. Sites constituting an Indian reserve or settlement were prohibited from occupation and acquisition.

As the best land was soon to be pre-empted by new settlers, the effect was to eventually restrict the native population to what previously had been only their wintering villages. The life of hunting and gathering was forced to change to agrarian. As the wintering villages were only required to be large enough to accommodate their abodes there was certainly not enough land set aside to grow hay or raise animals.

Children playing, Canoe Creek Reserve.

In the early 1870's, a joint Federal Provincial committee was established to address Indian matters in the province, creating reserve lands to be held in trust by the Federal government. There were constant arguments between the two branches of government regarding the size of reserves to be allotted; the Provincial officials insisted on 10 acres per family, whereas the Federal officials argued that 80 acres per family should be set aside. This was much less than the 160 acres allotted in the recent treaties on the Canadian Prairies.

Joe Bishop at the Indian Meadows.

The Canoe Creek reserve #1 was eventually surveyed and recorded on June 4th 1884 as 93 acres.

In her book "Victims of Benevolence" Elizabeth Furness wrote:

"....Yet as farming lands and water rights were overtaken by settlers, the agricultural subsistence was also becoming precarious. This was clearly the case with the Canoe Creek Band, as described by Obalate Father C. J. Grandidier in 1880:

'At Canoe Creek... The natives have not more than fifteen or twenty acres of land to support one hundred and fifty Indians. Their cattle are on the mountains; if they come down they are exposed to trespass, are seized, and not delivered until a fine has been paid. If the Indians need milk for their families they are obliged to go up the mountain for a mile, (carry) with them their cans, and take their milk down. When they want to cut wild grass for hay, to feed their horses and cattle in winter, the whites step in and claim the grass as their own. This state of things has lasted for many years'."

Although Father Grandidier was low on his estimation of the acres involved, the situation was correct, an extreme shortage of arable land existed all through the 1870's.

Chief William of the Williams Lake band outlined his tribe's plight and his frustration with the situation in a letter published in a 1879 Victoria Daily Colonist article:

"I am an Indian Chief and my people are threatened by starvation. The white men have taken all the land and all the fish. The country was ours. It is all gone. The noise of the threshing machine and wagon has frightened the deer and beaver. We have nothing to eat. We cannot live on the air and we must die. My young men are angry.... I do not know what to say next week when the chiefs assemble in council. A war with the white will end in destruction but death in war is not so bad as death by starvation. The land, which my people have lived on for 500 years, was taken by a white man; he has piles of wheat and cattle. We have nothing, not an acre. Another white man can take 320 acres of our land and the Indian dare not touch an acre.... Now what I want to say is this – there will be trouble sure. The whites have taken all the salmon and all the land and my people will not starve in peace."

Above: Louie Tinmusket's cabin at Indian Meadows before it was scavenged for the timber.
Left:: Louie Tinmusket , taken at Kamloops C-1912.

The situation was partially resolved by the Provincial Government in the early 1880s. Although pre-emptions and purchases had taken up the most desirable land, additional areas were added and by June of 1884 Canoe Creek in the official Plan Book in Victoria was;

Reserve #1   93 acres.

Reserve #2   4460 acres.

Reserve #3   6931 acres.

Today the Dog Creek and Canoe Creek bands have merged, with the administration office located in Dog Creek. The Canoe Creek Band web site estimates a band population of 650 with less than half living on the reserves in the two communities.

Canoe Creek Cabins.

The following four pages are copies of the original "Minutes Of Decision" on the Canoe Creek Reserve, July 21st 1881.

Minutes of Decision.

— Canoe Creek Indians —

— No. 1. —

<u>The old Reserve</u>, situated on Canoe creek, and containing 90 acres, is hereby reserved.

<u>One hundred (100) inches of water</u> is allotted from Canoe creek for the use of this reserve., &

¹⁶ (inches)

— No. 2. —

<u>A Reserve</u> of 4460 acres, situated on Canoe creek, 12 miles above Reserve No. 1.

Commencing at a fir tree, the South-eastern corner of Mr Van Volkenburgh's pro-perty, and running due East 120 chains; thence due South 80 chains; thence due East 330 chains; thence due South 140 chains; thence due West 80 chains; thence due North 100 chains; thence due West 370 chains, and thence due North 140 chains to place of commencement.

<u>The Water</u> flowing naturally through this land is reserved for the use of the Indians. <u>Also</u> the right to the <u>Waters</u> of "White Lake."

Canoe Creek Indians.

N° 2. — Continued.

lake", "Par ous", and "Park-sib-a-wis"
lakes, situated in the direction of the
70 mile house on the Cariboo waggon
road, with power to divert the same
through a low valley to this reserve.

N° 3.

A Reserve containing 5320 acres,
approximately, situated on the left
bank of Fraser river, 3 miles below
Dog Creek.

Commencing at a post on the left bank
of Fraser river on the Northern line of
Township 8, Lillooet district; thence due
East an approximate distance of 340,
chains, to the North-eastern corner of Section
31, Township 4; thence due North 160 chains;
thence due West an approximate distance
of 344 chains to the Fraser river; and thence
down the left bank of the said river to
the place of Commencement.

One hundred (100) inches of
Water is set apart for the use of this
reserve, to be taken from a small tributary
of Dog creek, which empties into it from
the South, a short distance above
Gaspards house.

N° 4.

Canoe Creek Indians.

— No. 4. —

A Reserve of 100 acres situated on the first creek below "Haines Creek", on the right bank of the Fraser; to include all Indian cultivation, and ditches in good survey shape.

Fifty (50) inches of Water are set apart from the creek flowing through this reserve for the use of the Indians.

— Fisheries. —

The exclusive right of fishing on both banks of Fraser river, from a point 1½ mile above the mouth of Canoe creek, down stream to a conical shaped rock in the middle of the river, a distance of about 5½ miles.

The right to fish in Green Lake, situated 4 miles East of the 73 mile post on the Cariboo waggon road.

— Burial Grounds. —

A Grave-yard situated on the left bank of Canoe Creek, ½ a mile from its mouth, marked by four stakes: 1 chain North and South, by 2 chains East and West.

Canoe Creek Indians.

— Burial Grounds — Cnt'd —

A Grave-yard to the South of the trail from Mr VanVolkenburgh's house to the mouth of Canoe creek, and about one mile distant from the latter, marked by four stakes, — 50 links North and South, by 50 links East and West.

A Grave-yard ½ mile West from Mr VanVolkenburgh's house, on the right bank of Canoe creek, and distant from it 2 chains, marked by four stakes, 140 links magnetic North and South, by 40 links magnetic East and West.

A Grave-yard situated in Mr VanVolkenburgh's timothy field, 7. chains North of Canoe creek, marked by four stakes, — 40 links due North and South, by 60 links East and West.

P. O'Reilly
I.R.C.

Canoe Creek B. C.
July, 21st 1881.

The Church

The Oblate Missionaries of Mary Immaculate arrived in Canoe Creek in 1867 and established the first church, St. Gabriel. The church was one of a series of ten that the Order had constructed from Soda Creek in the north to Seton Portage in the south. Services soon commenced and the first baptism recorded was on November 11th, 1867, baby Gertrude. The parents were father-Tichwasked, mother- Toattle-klallocks.

Williams Lake Tribune published the following article in 1985:

"One of these little churches was situated at Canoe Creek and was called St. Gabriel. Its remnants are still visible today.

But the little church fell prey to the ravages of time and weather. In 1897, Father F.M. Thomas, the dedicated priest who traveled throughout the Cariboo for over fifty years bringing Christ into the lives of its people, felt that a new church was needed at Canoe Creek.

Canoe Creek church of St. Paul, October 19th 1900.

Father Thomas met with the leaders of the community, then wrote in his memoirs later: "Within three hours, all the men had promised to donate $25.00 each towards the church, while each woman promised $5.00. Besides that, one promised to donate a cow, another a steer, another a pig, and someone promised five sacks of oats. The chief's wife promised to give away every calf born of her lone cow until the Church had been officially paid for. Tougan, a man of 85, gave his only horse, saying: "This is my only horse and all my bones are broken. Now I have neither horses nor legs but it is as the priest said, if I can help build a house for God here at Canoe Creek, the good God will give me his own house in Heaven".

Finally after two years, the church was finished and officially blessed and dedicated. The date was October 19th 1900.

Back- George Jim, unknown, Father Chippney, unknown, Father Thomas, Jimmy Brown (with hammer), front- Chief Johnny, William Adam.

"Despite the heroic efforts of Canoe Creek residents, the historic church of St. Paul – which had served the community for eighty five years – was destroyed by fire in the early hours of July 21st."

The blaze was first noticed by Rosie Seymour, who lives nearby with her husband, Gilbert. She was awakened at 6 a.m. by the smell of smoke, and discovered the front of the church in flames.

She tried to open the door to ring for help but the flames forced her away. She then screamed for help, and soon frantic villagers appeared with buckets.

Not only was the church on fire, but there was a very real danger of the fire spreading up into the hills which, because of the long hot weather, were tinder dry. In fact, the whole of the Canoe Creek valley could have gone up in flames. But enough water was packed by hand from the irrigation ditch to wet down the area surrounding the church, as well as the roof and walls of the Seymour house. This effort saved the house and the valley.

An early photo of the Seymours, Augustine, Old Stick (Johnny) Johnny (Crazy Johnny), and Basil.

Unfortunately, the church could not be saved. Within an hour, the old landmark was a mere pile of charred ruins and a few smouldering beams.

The dissappearance of the church is a great loss to the community, which is comprised of Canoe Creek Indians living in the village, along the valley and even into Clinton. The other half of the community consists of Jack and Shirley Koster and their family, whose ranch- the B.C. Cattle Company Ltd.- lies alongside the village in the beautiful valley.....

Despite sadness at the loss of their historic church, the Canoe Creek community and its sister community, Dog Creek, along with their new pastor, Father Guillet (OMI), are hoping that a new house of worship can be built before too long."

The new church, replacement for the historic place of worship that had been a major influence on the lives of the Canoe Creek valley residents.

These small outlying churches were visited by travelling priests, buggy in summer, sleigh in winter. The name most recognized in the south Cariboo was that of Father F.M. Thomas. Born in France, Father Francois Marie Thomas came to the already established St. Joseph's Mission, south of Williams Lake, in the spring of 1897. The mission had been established by the order of Obalates of Mary Immaculate as a residential and industrial school in order to facilitate the assimilation of the native children into the "accepted" society.

J. H. Blome, St Joseph's Mission Williams Lake   Ashcroft, B. C.
Cariboo

John Henry Blome, travelling photographer, took the above photo during the 1890s. Blome documented much of the history during the decade he operated in the south Cariboo. The original is in the Earl Cahill Collection.

Father Thomas served his parish for nearly six decades. Whenever the priest arrived on his circuit in these small outlying areas congregations would take the opportunity to have their children baptized and their marriages recognized and recorded. These events would be coordinated with the Fathers' trips.

Travelling Obalates not only served the native population but also stopped at places that might supply a meal and accommodation. The Riley ranch at Big Bar Creek was one of these and young Patricia Riley remembers Father Thomas's visits in the early 1920s:

"We always knew via "moccasin Telegraph" just when Father was on his way, but not the day or the time but we considered he was like Santa Claus and looked forward to his visit. This entailed making mud pies, some mixture of sawdust and mud being in the spring. We were sure he would enjoy our feeble effort. He arrived driving his horse and buggy and I can still see him all dressed in black even to his long cassock. Maybe as children our Santa Claus vision was due to his quite long beard but also the holy medals, books and pictures plus the large roll of very black licorice he brought. When we got through with his boisterous greeting and laughter we could not wait until he had nibbled at the mud pies and telling us how good they were. He was always happy and took such delight in our games as childish as they were, as I believe he was much more comfortable with children than with adults. In the afternoon mother would tell us to let Father go for his "alone" walk as he wanted to say his daily breviary and have a dip in the creek. In the winter time dad and Ernie Love used to cut a hole in the ice for him and remember them remarking on his toughness as there was no other person they knew who could or would do such a blood chilling way of bathing. He would only stay two or three days and then midst his great laugh and fond good-byes, he was away."

Pat wrote the following addendum with her feelings on Father Thomas: *"He was a great priest for those times and was always at home either with the Indians whom he loved or with the "White" people. At that time if it weren't for Father*

Thomas not an Indian or any Catholic would have been baptized. He was one of the great Obalate Missionaries of that time and era, long passed."

Above: Postcard from Father Thomas to Patricia In July of 1933. (With his Signature on the left side) Right: Pat Riley at the Riley Ranch C-1924.

Another of Pat's meomories is of Father Thomas at the dinner table where he would extract a small silver toothpick from his vest pocket and proceed to pick his teeth. However this small lapse of table etiquette did not in any way diminish the respect that she held for him. As I write this Pat is 91 years young and living in South Surrey.

Church of St. Paul Canoe Creek.

This photo is from Mary Palmantier's album. It was marked "Two girls at school about 1890". The centre girl (marked with an X) is identified on the back as Francois-Canoe Creek.

Unidentified girls at St. Joseph school concert.

St. Joseph school concert.
Back: #1, unidentified #2, Joe Dick, #3, Harry Dick
Front row: #1 Charlie Alphonse,3,4, & 5 unidentified #2, Matthew Dick.

Another Concert, #1 Rose Emile,#2 Katie Ross #3-Leona Isnardy, #4-Emma
Henry, #5-Nancy Tenale, #6- Alice Gilbert, #7-Annie Dasgal,
#8-Annie Dixon.

THE EARLY YEARS

When Lance Corporal Conroy drew his map of the Fraser in the summer of 1861, Canoe Creek was marked with only three buildings, two Indian Lodges and a trading post.

Although unidentified as the operators, the trading post was probably run by Robert P. Ritchie and his wife Sarah. The Ritchies never held official title to the property, but were fairly long time residents at Canoe Creek.

It was surely the Richies whom a young cowboy, Andrew Jackson Splawn, encountered at Canoe Creek in the spring of 1862. In 1861 Major John Thorpe had hired sixteen year old A.J. to help drive a herd of cattle from Yakima Valley Washington to the Cariboo goldfields. It was a slow and dangerous trip, encountering hostile natives and extreme weather. The end of the travelling season and they were at the Bonaparte River between Cache Creek and the Hat Creek. They wintered the cattle here and in the spring they again headed north.

Splawn wrote his memories of this trip in a book "Ka-mi-akin-The Last Hero of the Yakimas" The chapter was headed "The Cowboy of 1861".

His description of the Clinton - Canoe Creek portion is:

".... There we saw more ducks and geese in one-half hour than I have ever seen since. The whole country was covered with them during our four days' drive along this chain of lakes. The mouth of Canoe Creek on the Fraser was our next stop. The creek got its name from being the point where Simon Fraser of the North West Company, after descending the Fraser River to this place in 1807, cached his canoe and

traveled on foot to the site of Yale. Here we found a farmer with a herd of cows, and for the first time in eighteen months we had milk to drink, at the minimum cost of 25 cents a bowl."

Robert Skelton's book, "They Call it the Cariboo", included a section on frontier justice in which he wrote the following:

"….From time to time a lone miner on his way down the road would be robbed of his gold and sometimes killed. In 1865 (or 1866) a man called Morgan was found killed not far from Soda Creek. He had left the diggings with a heavy poke of gold and had been sporting a gold watch. Both the watch and the poke were missing. Some time later two Indians offered <u>Mrs. Ritchie of Canoe Creek</u> a gold watch and chain for sale. She suspected nothing for Indians were often paid for their services by gifts of this kind. After some bargaining, she bought the watch. Later, she realised that the watch might well have been Morgan's, and the two Indians, one from Lillooet and one from Nicomen were traced, questioned, and jailed in Quesnel to await trial. One day, however, the Nicomen Indian, who had until that moment been entirely peaceable, attacked his gaoler, Constable Sullivan, with a knife and nearly killed him before making his escape. The Lillooet Indian chose to stay where he was. The Nicomen crossed the border into the United States and Constable Richard Lowe of Osoyoos discovered that he had a girlfriend on the Canadian side whom he often visited. He bribed the other Indians to steal the Nicomen's rifle when he next called on the girl and they did so. Lowe surprised the Indian with his girl and captured him: placing him on horseback and handcuffing his ankles together under the horse's belly, he led his prisoner to Lytton, by way of Princeton, Coultee's, the Nicomen trail to the Thompson River, and, at last, the Wagon road, arriving in the middle of the night. From Lillooet his prisoner was sent to New Westminster where he joined his sometime companion of Lillooet. At the trial, held in Richfield, the Lillooet Indian turned state's evidence and was given a life sentence. The Nicomen Indian was sentenced to death. Although the watch was recovered the poke was never recovered, and it became part of a local legend that somewhere along Morgan Creek, (for the creek was inevitably named after the murdered man) that a poke of gold is still hidden…."

The Federal Government opened a post office at Canoe Creek July 1st 1873, appointing Robert P. Richie as postmaster.

Robert's wife Sarah passed away unexpectedly, with a sudden heart attack in July 1874. She was only 46. Robert was left to continue the operation in Canoe Creek as postmaster and trader. The post office was closed permanently on April 1st 1879.

An early photo of some Canoe Creek Cattle.

Beginning of the Beef.

Although the Ritchies had cattle at Canoe Creek the real business of raising stock began in earnest when the Van Volkenburg family made a deal with Robert. The land encompassing the buildings of Canoe Creek was surveyed in 1875. At this time the ranch had four buildings shown and the reserve had four, one of which would be the new Church.

Benjamin Van Volkenburgh applied for and received a crown grant for two large parcels of land in June 1884; these were to become the beginning of the future B.C. Cattle Company land holdings.

The Van Volkenburgh name is not normally associated with the early cattle business in B.C. Benjamin, Abraham & Isaac were Americans of German lineage who arrived early and became associated with the more famous Harper Brothers, Jerome and Thaddeus. It would seem to be a natural, Harpers having an outlet for their beef and Van Volkenburghs a steady supply of beef for their markets. The Hibbens directory of 1871 shows "Harper and Van Volkenburg Meat Market" listed in Yale. Ten years later in the 1881 Census Abraham (butcher) and his wife Dora were still in the meat business in Yale.

Isaac Van Volkenburgh

Benjamin, also a butcher, ran the Victoria operation. Isaac was running the cattle operation in Canoe Creek with the help of three Chinese. Moy Ah was listed as "labourer" and Toy Ah and Tiate Ah were listed as "Cattle Raiser". The relationship between the Harpers and Van Volkenburghs would continue until the eventual demise of the Harper Empire in 1888.

During the early 1870's Jerome Harper decided to retire and move to California where he died in December 1874. His brother Thaddeus was the beneficiary of Jerome's will and this was the beginning of his expansion of the Harper Holdings. It was after Jerome's death that Thaddeus and the Van Volkenburghs became even more financially entwined.

In the summer of 2007 a most interesting event occurred. The basement of the Clinton Government building yielded two boxes (duplicates) of original documents executed by Clinton's first government agent, Frederick W. Soues. These papers consisted of bills of sales, mortgages, promissory notes and other notarised papers, giving insight into some of the earliest legalised transactions in the Clinton area. I had the opportunity to review these papers before they were shipped off to Victoria to be preserved. Some pertained to the Harpers and Van Volkenburghs.

Document #139 (Box #2) – Recorded April 18th 1871.
Record of Conveyance. Most references to the Harper's Lumber and Gristmill in Clinton indicate that Harper did not actually own the property. This document lays to rest any argument as it conveys the property (adjoining the Connish Farm) purchased from J.H. Scott to Jerome Harper.

Document #130 – dated November 11th 1879.
This was a thirteen-page loan agreement between Charles Edward Pooley, Thaddeus Harper and Benjamin Van Volkenburgh. The asset pledged was 4000 head of cattle at Harper's California Gasper Creek Ranch. The amount was $25,000.00. Thaddeus was living at the Clinton Mills.

Jerome Harper, C-1865.

Document #139 – Dated May 3rd 1880.

This was a four-page letter by Thaddeus Harper and Benjamin Van Volkenburgh to their credit grantors in Victoria requesting permission to relocate the grist and lumber mill to the mouth of the Bonaparte River.

Two early photographs of Harper's Grist Mill at The mouth of the Bonaparte River.

Document #175 – Dated May 19th 1882.

Bill of Sale between the Van Volkenburgh brothers and J.B. Greaves for the sale of 400 two-year-old steers at Canoe Creek for $18.00 per head.

Document #187 – Dated April 21st 1884.

Loan agreement between the Van Volkenburgh brothers, Isaac and Benjamin and Chas. E. Pooley of Victoria for $5000.00. The asset pledged was 1500 head of sheep and lambs that were running on Big Bar mountain.

Document # 192 – Dated June 20th 1884.

Mortgage taken by Benjamin (residing in Victoria) and Isaac (residing in Canoe Creek) Van Volkenburgh in the amount of $67,028.00. Because of the large size of this mortgage it is likely that Harper was involved to some degree. Thaddeus Harper became overextended in the mid 1880s and his empire was forced into receivership in 1888. It was around this time that the Van Volkenburghs also decided to wind up their operations in Canoe Creek with the sale to a new syndicate, "The B.C. Cattle Company Limited".

An original stock certificate from the authors collection.

Three partners, Mr. John Irving, Mr. Thomas Ellis and Mr. Richard Lowe Cawston incorporated the British Columbia Cattle Company Ltd. on November 5th, 1890. It was formed for the purpose of *"to carry on farming, stock raising and butchering and to acquire land for that purpose". The company managed the Triangle Ranch at Quilchena as well as the Canoe Creek operation.*

Richard Lowe Cawston

Cawston arrived in B.C. in 1874 settling in the southern Okanagan. He managed the Lowe-Haynes cattle operation in Osoyoos until 1884 when he moved to Keremeos. He is well remembered for vaccinating the local natives en masse during a small pox epidemic. One of the original partners in 1890, he relinquished his shares to take his family back to Ontario for their education. This completed, the family returned to British Columbia where he died in Cawston on July 23rd 1923.

The town of Cawston adopted the name in 1954 in recognition of his family.

Mr. Thomas Ellis C-1890

The eldest in an Irish family of seventeen and with few prospects at home, Tom Ellis left for Canada and arrived in Penticton at the young age of nineteen on the 25th of May 1865. He pre-empted land in 1869 and was the first non-native settler. He and his wife Wilhemina had nine children and became very successful in the cattle industry. The Triangle ranch at Quilchena and the Canoe Creek ranch were part of this empire.

Captain John Irving

John Irving was the secretary of the B.C.C.C. and headquartered in Victoria. Captain John came to Vancouver with his parents in 1858. He took over his father's Pioneer Line shipping in 1872 and in 1883 amalgamated it with the Hudson's Bay Line to form The Canadian Pacific Navigation Co. He represented the Cassiar District in the B.C. Legislature from 1894 to 1901. Captain J. Irving was always regarded as a giant of the steamboat industry in British Columbia.

Robert Patterson Rithet

Rithet's history was in shipping, and he was involved in the B.C.C.C. only as an investment. President of Welch & Co. he had offices in San Francisco California and Victoria, B.C.. Rithet knew the intricacies of the cattle business, as he had been Thaddeus Harper's business agent both in Victoria and California.

With Cawston's and Ellis's expertise in the management of cattle and the business support of Captain John Irving and eventually Robert Rithet, the B.C. cattle Company was underway. Now with the assets of the Van Vaulkenburgs in Canoe Creek in new hands, a manager for the ranch was hired.

The census for 1891 lists the manager as Dominque Ercole, a single man born in France. Assisting him in the operation of the ranch were Ah Pong, labourer and Lee Po listed as cook. He was still listed as the manager in the Williams directory for 1893.

By 1895 the Williams directory listed ranch manager Duncan Patterson, with John R. Williams from Dog Creek as labourer. Patterson was born in Ontario in 1860. He continued as manager until the company hired John Lowther, a farmer from Clinton.

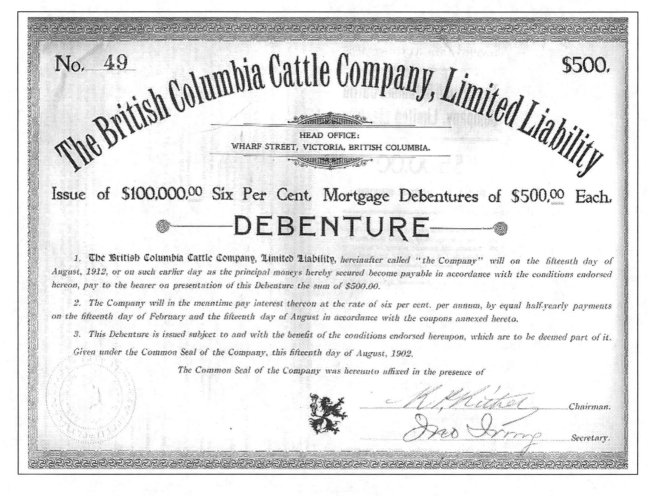

An original debenture document signed by John Irving, secretary.

THE LOWTHERS

Born in Perth Ontario on January 14th 1847, John James Lowther was 30 years old when he came to British Columbia. The 1881 census shows him in Soda Creek and according to Lowther family history he is driving either stages or freight wagons to Barkerville.

John and his Irish wife, Marianne (Minnie) Stedmond had six children: Jane (Jenny) born 1888 in Quesnel; Eliza (Iza) born 1890 in Clinton; Alice Geraldine, Clinton 1891; Mary Louise (May), Clinton 1896; Eileen; and William (Bill) born at Canoe Creek in June 1900. Birth certificates for the children born in Clinton list John as "rancher" residing in Clinton. Sometime during the 1890's John was hired by the British Columbia Cattle Company as manager of their operation at Canoe Creek, B.C. He continued in this capacity until his retirement in 1909. The family then moved to Nanaimo where they opened the "Lowther Boarding House".

During their stay in Canoe Creek John wrote to John Irving, the secretary of the B.C. Cattle Co., on a bi-weekly basis reporting conditions and circumstances at the ranch. Most reports are mundane, however certain excerpts warrant quoting.

Marianne (Minnie) Lowther.

**Eileen, Bill, Jenny, May and Iza at Canoe Creek, B.C..
The children attended school in a one-room schoolhouse,
probably on the ranch. After completion of her studies,
Jenny assumed the teaching responsibilities.**

John's most serious problems in managing the ranch were the weather, shortage of reliable help and the poor relationship between the Company and the natives on the Canoe Creek reserve.

Water for irrigation purposes had never been in abundant, controllable amounts and approval had been issued to re-construct the dam on the creek. Water usage was the cause of some of the friction existing between the natives and the ranch. The attitude of the ranch is shown in the following report.

Report of August 6th, 1903

"….Re Dam. We will put it in as good repair as possible with the material on hand and also beg to suggest that the Canoe Creek Indians be not allowed to do any work on the dam as this ranch requires all of the water and these Indians insist on taking out enough water to irrigate the whole reserve. As the Company have the water rites they

should do their own work on the dam and any water they may give the indians should be given as a gratuity and not as a right- these people have caused us trouble every season by taking the water when the Company's own crop requires it and before I summon anybody to court I want to be sure that I am in the right. Their labor amounts to very little anyway...."

Report of September 10th, 1904

"....I have written twice in the last month to A. (Alonzo) Tresierra, who runs a little sawmill on the Big Bar Creek, for three inch planks for the sluice way in the dam. I got a reply this mail saying he could furnish them at fourteen dollars per thousand feet. I have written him this mail to cut them at once and if he would deliver them at the Dog Creek road on top of Big Bar Mountain, I would allow him five dollars per thousand more...."

Report of December 17th, 1904;

"....Two Indians, Crazy Johnnie and Lincoln worked two days on the dam in

November. They refuse to accept their time checks for this work, so I am sending

Reliable Canoe Creek cowboys.
Louie, Augustine & Basil Seymour.

the account, three dollars each, to Mr. Bell, the Indian Agent, this mail. These Indians evidently think by refusing pay for their work, it will give them a claim on the water..."

The marketing of cattle from the ranch was done in Victoria, a Partnership, "The B.C. Market Co.", had been formed in the meat market business between the B.C. Cattle Co. and Western Canadian Ranching Co. The Market Co. advised the dates they would require carload shipments and John would make up a cattle drive to the railhead at Ashcroft. Dependable help was seldom available.

Report of August 20th, 1904;

"....Should the B.C. Market Co. require any cattle from Canoe Creek before the

last of October I wish you would see Mr. Welch and arrange with him to send up a reliable person to take charge of the cattle. It is impossible for me to leave the ranch for eight or nine days and I don't want to trust the Indians after the bungling they made with the last drive...."

Report of April 23rd, 1904

"....We put a third team to work yesterday, up till then we had been working two teams. It is hard to get men who can drive a team, I am working one Siwash and four Chinamen at present."

There were natives that were dependable. Philip Boston, Johnnie Naw Naw, Willie Boston and Indian George were examples of repeated hires.

Philip Boston at Canoe Creek.

Lowther relied on the Canoe Creek chief, Copper Johnny, to take charge and supervise the drives to Ashcroft:

"He is the most reliable Indian here and I allowed him fifty cents per day more than the others and full time till he returned as an inducement to him to handle the cattle carefully and see that no mistakes were made...."

Even Copper Johnny did not always perform as Lowther would have liked as he wrote:

"....They also lost four steers between Raphael's and Beaver Dam and came back to White Lake and replaced them with four light steers that should be kept over. Indians and Chinamen are the only help to be had in this section and if I go to Ashcroft with the beef drives the work on the Ranch must be stopped till I return or there will be little done so under the circumstances there appears to be no help for such blundering."

Chinese were the ranch's main supply of permanent labor and were used as cooks, domestics, irrigators and laborers. The 1901 Census listed three staying at the ranch in March, Ah Jun, laborer, Ah Kit laborer, and Ah Lum, cook.

In addition over the years covered in the reports, Ah Yen, Ah Jim #3 and Ah Hop #5 Cook were some of the Chinese employed. Others were only referred to as Chinamen.

Wages were $1.50 per day during branding and round up and haying, and $1.00 per day on off-season work. The wage structure was the same for natives and Chinese.

Also a subject of many reports to the Secretary in Victoria was the weather. The May 18th report of 1901 included the following:

"A cyclone visited the Gang Ranch on Thursday last and made a complete wreck of their floom and leaves the ranch without water.

This floom was ¾ of a mile long and over fifty feet high and took two seasons to build."

The Gang Ranch Flume circa 1880's, destroyed by high winds, May 1901.

The fourth manager of the Canoe Creek division of the B.C. Cattle Co. was Allan Lincoln Calhoun Hannon. Born March 3rd 1866 in Waco Texas, known as Link, he brought with him to British Columbia a part of the true Wild West. Stories of the Old West that were popular at the time in the "dime" pulp magazines were only a copy of his early life, in print.

Harry Marriott in his book "Cariboo Cowboy" described Hannon:

"Hannon was a real capable ranch manager and very little ever got by his attention. He was a number one cattleman, and could size up a bunch of cattle better than most ranchers I knew in that area. Neat and tidy, the ranch buildings and fences

were always kept in good shape. He spoke with that Southern Texas drawl, always more or less a silent type of fellow- but once in a while he'd break loose and tell me of his boyhood days in Texas. It sure was interesting to hear him tell of some of those well known characters of the south, and the early cattle drives from Texas as far north as the state of Montana."

Audrey Higbee, (Philip and Nancy Grinder's great granddaughter) of Washington State, has been instrumental in most of the research on Lincoln's early history. In the book "Remembering Robert's Creek" it mentioned that he was only twelve when leaving his father's home on the Rio Grande River. Apparently two strangers hired him to be their cook and later he heard that one of them was Billy the Kid. From cooking he turned to being a cowboy,

Lincoln Calhoun Hannon

herding longhorns north from Texas over the Chisholm Trail.

Author David Peck wrote the following history of Link Hannon in the Lovell Chronicle for June 28th 2007-Mustang Days. The headline was:

"Dry Head shootout took place".

"One of the last areas of the "wild, wild West" in the United States was the Big Horn Basin of Wyoming and the Dry Head area of southern Montana just to the northeast of Lovell."

About 105 years ago, frontier justice and the modern justice system came together in a story researched by Chris Finlay. - a story of a pioneer cowboy named Link Hannon that includes a battle over grazing, a shootout, a sheriff and a posse.

Lincoln Hannon (white shirt) with his mostly native round-up crew at the Canoe Creek ranch. In "Cariboo Cowboy", Harry Marriott described them: *"The ranch always had an entirely Indian crew, with a Chinese cook and two Chinese irrigators ...The Indian boys mostly belonged to the Indian Village ... they were a real capable bunch as far as ranch work goes and most of them quiet and slow-spoken."*

.... Hannon had trailed cattle to the Dry Head from Texas in the late 19ᵗʰ century and "picked a hell of a good spot" to settle down, squatting on land near Davis Creek....

Hannon built at least one cabin and had twenty acres of irrigated grass hay "a feat in itself back then".

In those days there were no fences in the area, which was common in that time period. Another early pioneer, Frank Strong also moved some cattle into the Dry Head area at the Ewing Ranch, and some of the cattle eventually worked their way north to Davis Creek and Hannon's hayfield".

Rosa Vida Bischoff Black in "Lovell our Pioneer Heritage" wrote an account of what followed.

"His neighbours Mr. Hannon and Harry Mogan weren't fond of the idea. So the first time he saw some of Strong's cattle in the Dry Head, they cut out 28 head and headed them across the green rolling hills toward the gorge.

Running in a frenzy to get away from the harassment behind them, the poor animals were at the brink of the chasm before they could comprehend the peril – or hope to stop – and so they plunged helplessly down the hundreds of feet....

Angry about what happened, Strong organised some men to go and confront

A very dapper, Louie Vedan.

Hannon, and the result of the confrontation was about a five - hour gunfight, that took place on July 1ˢᵗ 1902."

An early Bridger Montana newspaper account put it this way, the story appearing under the headline ***"More trouble in the Dry Head"***

"Another open rupture occurred in the Dry Head district last Wednesday between Messrs. Hannon and Mogan on the one side and Messrs. Strong, Morris, et al on the other. The first reports of the affair were rather fierce, but later it was found only to be an ordinary shooting that has occurred so often in that notorious locality for the past several years, and the five hour desperate battle resulting in two men killed and several wounded and the Hannon gang fortified among the rocks of the Big Horn river, and all that, has been toned down to one man (Morris) actually shot and wounded, and Messrs. Hannon and Mogan submitting themselves peacefully to sheriff Potter."

An arrest warrant for Hannon and Mogan was signed by the sheriff on July 3ʳᵈ and executed on the next day. The charges were – *"that they did unlawfully, wilfully, maliciously and feloniously with intent to kill a human being, commit an assault upon one Ed Morris with loaded firearms, deadly weapons likely to produce death, to-wit rifles, loaded with gunpowder and leaden bullets… did shoot at and wound the person of Ed Morris…."*

The result of the trial was an acquittal for both Hannon and Mogan, as the jury brought in a verdict of "Not Guilty".

"Hannon got into trouble again in 1904, first facing charges of forging a bill of sale in district court in Basin, then charged with grand larceny in Red Lodge for supposedly robbing and looting the sluice boxes of G.W. Barry's Hidden Canyon Gold Mines.

The June 10ᵗʰ 1904, Bridger Free Press account of the Montana charges called Hannon "the Dry Head rancher who has gained considerable notoriety on account of having been arrested several times on various charges " but went on later to say "One peculiar thing about these arrests of Hannon is the fact that he has thus far been acquitted of every charge upon which he has been tried."

The article in the Chronicle concluded with: *"Was Link Hannon a notorious scoundrel who stampeded cattle off a cliff, then shot a local man who came to confront him, or was he merely defending his turf and was justified in his actions? Historian Edwin C. Bearss in a history of the Big Horn Canyon area described Hannon and Mogan as "Two local toughs".*

Regardless of the answer to the last question, Link Hannon felt it was time to move on. By 1906 Lincoln was working for the B.C. Cattle Company in the Nicola Valley. When it was time for John Lowther and family to retire to the coast, the position of ranch manager in Canoe Creek was given to Hannon.

Lincoln and his roundup crew at cow camp, possibly at what they referred to as the Chilcotin Ranch in Empire Valley. Fred Boyle, photographer, took the photo.

The 1911 census listed Lincoln, his son Thompson, three boarders, two domestics (employees) and Emma Vedan with two of her children, James and Ellen. Mrs. Vedan was listed as housekeeper.

Early pioneers, Philip Grinder and Nancy Kastalamarx.

Emma was the youngest daughter of Philip and Nancy Grinder and had married Louie Vedan in 1896. Louis Vedan has been written about elswhere, never complimentary, in regards to the treatment of his animals. Apparently this also applied to his family. Eventually Emma and her four children packed up and left, arriving in Canoe Creek about 1910. The housekeeper relationship between Lincoln and herself eventually changed and although not married, Emma eventually became known as Mrs. Hannon.

The cattle business at this time was exceptional and in the annual report for 1915 it was noted they owned 17,000 to 18,000 acres of crown granted realestate and were running about 1200 head of cattle. This included 18 pedigree bulls recently purchased. The report stated: *"The herd is cross between shorthorn and hereford, and is said to be the best grade of cattle in British Columbia excepting the Douglas Lake Co.'s herd.*

The ranch buildings have all been renewed in the last four years, including a new dwelling house just completed at a cost of $4000.00. All this work has been paid for out of

Louie and Emma Vedan with two unidentified friends.

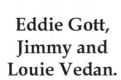

Eddie Gott, Jimmy and Louie Vedan.

Louie Vedan (on horse) with Placida and Marc Pigeon.

The new house under construction, 1914. The labour for the building was contracted to William Mason, General Contractor in Vancouver, for a total of $1400.00 plus transportation of crew to and from Clinton. Room and board to be supplied at $4.50 per employee per week during construction. Lincoln certified it as satisfactory and complete on March 27th 1915.

revenue including the purchase of a portable sawmill. There is a full line of implements on the ranch, in fact everything is in first class order."

The balance sheet for the year that ended on May 31st 1915 showed a total of retained earnings for the ranch of $38,000.00 of which $22,000.00 had been earned in the previous 12 months. Lincoln's bonus for the year was $411.85.

Hannon's Montana reputation obviously did not follow him to the Cariboo as the report continues:

"About four or five years ago Mr. Luke Hannon was appointed foreman on the ranch. Mr. Ellis is general manager of the Company but does not reside on the property although he visits it periodicaly. Mr. Hannon is an exceptionaly good man and since he has been on the place he has improved the property in every way. Practicaly the whole of the buildings have been replaced under his management, the herd has been improved by the purchase of pedigree bulls and is increasing yearly. The whole ranch has been fenced, a sawmill has been installed which brings in a small revenue besides cutting lumber for the ranch. All this work has been paid for of revenue and the Company has been able to pay not less than 8% dividends. From now on the dividends will increase yearly as all the improvements are completed and the herd is increasing yearly, and there does not seem to be any probability of a drop in the price of cattle for some time to come."

The company followed all the new construction with a general store. The opening inventory was extensive (cost $1172.00) and directed to the needs of the natives on the reserve. Drygoods ranging from - longjohns to mackinaws, medicines - Castor oil, epsom salts, enos fruit salts, Syrup of White Pine and eclectic oil. Tobacco - cigarettes (singles), Virginia Cut tobacco, Old Chum (pouches), McDonalds smoking, Cigars, and McDonalds chewing. Stock room items were as large as one ton of course salt and as small as a package of pins and even included a pail of hard candy to entice the children. One of Emma's chores was to look after the store and she supplied it with her own handicraft, handmade beaded buckskin gloves.

Emma Vedan, storekeeper at Canoe Creek store.

Joe Sargent, displaying a pair of Emma's gloves.

The new house after completion. C-1915. It was considered
by the shareholders to be one of the best, if not the best,
ranch house in the Cariboo.

C-1925. The sawmill in the field (center right), the white church on the
reserve. (upper right).

Lincoln and the ranch enjoyed a most prosperous time during the years of the"Great War". The demand for beef and the price had remained high for the duration of the conflict.

A daughter, Beaunie, was born to Emma and Lincoln in Kamloops on the 21st of April 1917.

Lincoln's deteriorating health made it necessary for him to resign. The family moved to Robert's Creek on the Sunshine Coast for him to recuperate. Francis George (Frank) Ellis took over the overall management of the ranch. Frank was the son of founding partner Tom Ellis. Looking for a foreman for the Canoe Creek ranch, Frank visited Harry Marriott at the Gang Ranch field on Big Bar mountain and offered him the position. Harry accepted and agreed to stay until December to complete

Lincoln, Emma and Beaunie.

roundup and have everthing prepared for the winter before leaving for his homestead on the Big Bar Lake.

On June 30th 1919 Tom Ellis purchased a new Dodge car from dealer, F.L. Peters in Ashcroft for $1850.00 and charged it to the ranch.

Circumstances were not as favorable for Frank, as it seemed that everything was against him. Beef prices had dropped, summers were dry and winters cold and stormy. As with previous managers, Frank made his reports to the secretary in Victoria every two weeks. Some interesting excerps describe the situation:

March 20th 1920

"…. *The spring is turning out very bad so far, real cold and backward almost like*

January. It is going to make things bad after starting so early last fall. Everyone expected an early spring. It is hard on hay and real bad for the breeding stock. Everyone in this district is tired of the long winter…. I understand Hannon is working for Hammond on the Basque Ranch near Ashcroft. He must be feeling younger already. I hear he was pretty sick with the change he made. He found it very expensive and was glad to get back to the upper country…."

Jimmy Vedan, Helen Nellie Vedan, Sadie Vedan, Beaunie Hannon and Emma Vedan (nee Grinder).

April 10th 1920:

"…. It has been an awful spring here. The worst in the history of the country I think. Yesterday and today have been our first spring days. Down to zero before that and one snowstorm following another. I think we will come out all right compared with others although the loss may be slightly above average. I don't think it will cripple us…."

Securing a sufficient supply of laborers was also a problem for Frank. He had traveled as far afield as Kamloops trying to acquire a crew:

"…. I had to pay Chinamen $80.00 per month and hard to get at that so am doing with two instead of three as usual. Wages are awful the Indians all want $75.00 per month now. God knows where it is all going to end. It is no snap running a ranch now a days I can tell you…."

Conditions remained the same for the winter of 1921-22. Frank advised they had no more hay and even the Gang was not in a position to let them have any more.

February 19th 1922:

"…. The winter keeps on with unabated fury. More like the North Pole than anywhere else. It is one succession of snowstorms followed by very severe cold snaps without any mild weather between and has no appearance of change. I have never seen a worse winter not even 1906-07 when I was in Alberta. Lots of cattle are dying on the feed grounds everywhere in spite of plenty to eat. They are frozen to death…. I am doing the best I can but it almost seems to be hopeless. It looks more like the polar regions than any place I know. The snow and ice is banked up to the tops of the fences in places…"

Finally on March 4th 1922 Frank's advice to the directors was:

"…. The cattle business is finished here while these dry seasons last. When the B.C. Cattle Co.'s winter range is finished growing anything they will have lost their biggest asset…. I have done my best against great odds and hope the next man will have better luck…."

March 17th 1922:

"…. It is the same as midwinter here yet, lots of snow and freezing very

hard. I fear this is the end of ranching on a large scale for the B.C. Cattle Co. for the present at any rate…. It would be better to sell the cattle and lease the place while things are in the present condition, if it were possible to get enough to pay the taxes etc. by leasing…."

Above: Eddie Haller, demonstrating his roping skills to his fellow soldiers in W.W.1 First cousin to the Vedan children, he sent this postcard to the family at Canoe Creek.

Right: : Isabelle showing her ability with the rope. Note the bundles of shingles on the roof ready for application. Also the store was under construction.
C-1914.

May 4th 1922:

"…. The River ranch is very bad and we have hardly any water enough for half our land. It is getting on now and we ought to get together this month and decide with the directors what we are going to do. It is a case of going out of cattle altogether and resting the range or carrying about 400 or 500 cattle instead of over 1100. I would suggest getting rid of all the cattle and trying sheep, which I understand Mr. Koster our neighbour is doing…. I am quite willing to let somebody else try their hand at ranching here as I have had a pretty strenuous time here and will not shed any tears at parting with The Canoe Creek Ranch….'

Unknown to Frank, Lincoln Hannon had applied for position as manager on April 29th 1922 for a salary of $135.00 per month. When Frank heard the news it resulted in the following spirited response:

May 12th 1922:

I received yours of April 29th yesterday on my return from rounding up the cattle and turning them out of the winter range. I immediately wired you that I objected on behalf of the Ellis estate to Hannon and Co. being put back on the ranch. I am also lodging a protest with the trustees of the Ellis estate to that effect. I am not casting any reflection on Hannon's ability as a stockman or rancher but I am objecting very strongly to the connections he carries with him. In the first place he is keeping a woman with a notorious bad character whose two brothers, John and James Grinder have both served terms in the penitentiary for stealing cattle and horses and in the past have operated on the range our cattle run on. John Grinder being employed by Hannon frequently when Hannon was here before.

The so-called Mrs. Hannon's brand (EV on right hip) was used promiscuously and her stock was wintered on the ranch here with our stock using our feed. Hannon's actions finally got so conspicuous that my father heard he had sold 60 head of cattle in one bunch so he got me to come up and investigate. When I arrived here quite unexpectedly, to Hannon, found 22 head of weaned year old bull calves running on our range without a mark or brand on them of any description. All were bulls so apparently were picked out as the easiest stock to market. These were turned loose in the month of April when there was no excuse for not branding them. All stockmen brand their calves (not branded in the fall on account of cold weather) as soon as it gets warm in March and before they are turned out of the feed ground. These undoubtedly were to be picked up by whoever was using this EV brand in the interests of the so-called Mrs. Hannon. John Grinder, ex-convict, her brother was at that time employed by Hannon on the ranch. He had previously served five years in the penitentiary for stealing cattle from our neighbour Thomas Derby of Crows Bar Ranch.

**Johnny and Jimmy Grinder – standing
Johnny Kostering – seated. C-1896.**

When my father heard what I said about my investigations he immediately wrote Hannon that he was to discontinue branding any cattle on his own a/c and that there were to be no stock except those belonging to the B.C. Cattle Co. kept on the ranch. Hannon replied that he was disposing of all his stock and would keep no outside cattle on the ranch. He claimed he was purchasing them from the Indians I found out since he bought about one percent of them from the Indians and the other 99 percent must have been stolen or born with the EV brand on them !!!

Big Bar Store, C-1909
1.) Johnny Grinder, 2) Jimmy Grinder, 3)Philip Grinder, 4) Billy Grinder, 5) Johanna Grinder, 6)Henry Grinder, 7) Joseph Tresierra, 8) Alonzo Tresierra, 9) Laura Tresierra, 10) Charles Kostering, 11) Dan Smith.

About one year later another mysterious brand appeared on the range amongst our cattle. It was called the tree brand (T). When I came up here four years ago I saw a bunch of these cattle running with our cattle on the winter range. I asked Hannon who owned the tree brand and he said it was an Indian brand and I bought those cattle from them the other day. On making further inquiries I found out the brand was made here for Hannon himself he having previously used the same brand in Montana where I may mention he also got into serious difficulties and had to make a hasty exit.

I found out also out of that bunch of cattle branded with a tree brand he had bought one from the Indians and about 15 were pick ups. The inference is that although Hannon may not have been doing the actual work himself the relatives of his woman were and he must have been sharing in the profits, as he knew what was going on. I quite admit Hannon had good luck when he was on Canoe Creek ranch before but conditions are totally different now and he knows it. He proved himself no farmer when he was here but depended entirely on the winter range which was in good shape then and he never had a hard winter all the time he was here. Were he here last winter he would have done the same as anybody else bought hay or lost the cattle. Any of the neighbours will bear me out in this.

Since he left us nobody seems to have tried very hard to get him as ranch manager. His name has been mentioned in connection with several places which needed good managers but upon making inquiries into details I noticed they have all dropped him from their list.

I feel satisfied the B.C. Cattle Co. were not aware of the real facts when they proposed putting Hannon back and I feel quite satisfied they will change their minds when they know the character of this woman and her relatives. Any of this information will bear investigation in the courts if it were necessary.
I may mention I am perfectly willing to stay here until some better prospect turns up in the way of manager. I think he ought to be honest, as there is no check on him way up here especially with the livestock. This is only a part of their history and I am not going any further as it is too lengthy in detail."

Even though Frank was a beneficiary of the Ellis estate and one would think his recommendation would carry considerable weight, not so, as the directors decided to override him and re-hire Lincoln. Frank had been fairly accurate in his appraisal of Emma's brothers Johnny and James. Johnny had been convicted of "Cattle Stealing" from Tom Derby. His trial was held in the little brick courthouse at Clinton May 30th 1902. The jury brought in a verdict of guilty and Johnny was sentenced to three years and six months in the B.C. Penitentiary.

Johnny and Melanie Grinder's family at Big Bar.
Back row: Annie, Mildred
Center row: Walter, Joe,
Front: Jimmy, Tina, Hector and Johnny.

Brother Jimmy is another story. His problems with the law seem to have culminated in 1907. Chief Constable W.L. Fernie at Kamloops wrote the following letter to The Superintendent of Police in Victoria on April 10th 1907:

"I am enclosing a letter which was handed to me to-day by Mr. V.D. Curry of Campbell Creek who had a saddle stolen by Jimmy Grinder when he left here. I think this

was written and addressed originally to Paul Stevens who has sent it anonymously to Curry, probably being afraid of being implicated by harboring Grinder….

This Jimmy Grinder is a regular scourge to this Upper Country which he knows thoroughly and in which he is more or less well liked by a certain stamp of men who assist him – he is young tall and good looking and a very good rough rider and I think one of the greatest horse thieves of his time. His arrest and punishment would be very popular with all the big cattlemen up here – there are several charges of horse stealing against him here, and one in Ashcroft.

If it is possible to extradite him I hope in this case it will be done as it is a very easy matter to slip across the Boundary line south of here, and there is an impression here that some horses disappear every year in this way.

The following is the best description I can get of Jimmy Grinder – Age 27 years. Height 6ft. 1 in. Hair – black. Eyes – dark brown. Complexion – dark. Religion – R.C. Nationality – B.C. half breed. Proportion – medium. Weight about 176 lb. Small moustache. Large scar between thumb and index finger left hand. Blotched face. Space between upper teeth big, one tooth gone on right. Round face. Reads and writes. Single. Intemperate. Has been in gaol. Cowboy, has ridden for "Buffalo Bill's Show".

Signed: W.L. Fernie, Chief Constable.

The letter that Fernie enclosed was hand written by Jimmy and the post mark was April 1907. Parts are illegible but some excerpts follow:

"…. Well Paul we get a good job here in the sale stables braking horses to drive I get $85.00 and board myself so I clear about $60.00 a month…. I suppose they was hot after me when I left. I raised hell on the road as I came I struck Bruster (Brewster) Wash. I had 6 dam good saddle horses – and I sold them and still got some of the money and having a good time every night.

Paul it is hell but shit it is all right…. How is my wife Mary is she get a kid yet. Say Paul talk about girls --I guess the Indian aint getting the girls. They all come my way so good-by you old sweed. From your Ever Truly Friend, James Grinder".

Jimmy had no conscience as to where he acquired his stock. In a disposition dated April 26th 1907, Joseph Haller advised that he suspected Jimmy of stealing a dark gray horse and four others off his property. Joseph Haller was Jimmy's brother in law. To dispose of the animals, Jimmy drove them south to Upper Hat Creek where he had the nerve to trade them to another brother in law, Tom Pocock. A warrant for Jimmy Grinder was issued on May 6th 1907, too late, for he was already south of the border. Jimmy returned at least once to the Big Bar area before returning to the U.S. and settling in Montana.

These two postcards were in James Vedan's album.
The rider is identified as James Grinder and the inscription in pencil on the right is , "James Grinder rough riding Buffalo Bill, see...."

James Grinder. Photo was taken on the Flathead Reservation in Montana, June 1909.

Before leaving the ranch Frank sent a rather derogitory report to Victoria that revealed his feelings towards the natives and the Gang Ranch.

"…. I will cut the wages as soon as the hay is finished. I never pay any attention to what the Gang Ranch do re. wages. I feel quite certain that the BCCC do not wish me to run this outfit on the lines of the Gang Ranch as we would soon be broke if I hired 5 men to do one man's work. It is commonly known throughout the country that the workmen all have their siesta behind the haycocks every afternoon. The manager is never there attending to business not at any time of the year and the Indians will not work here for the same money as they say I am around too much looking after them. Not wanting in any way to cast any slur on Stobie but I never saw any outfit trying to go broke quicker than the Gang Ranch are doing. Kindly do not repeat anything I have said re. the Gang Ranch as I don't want to hurt Holland's feelings…."

Frank Ellis turned the reins back over to Lincoln in the summer of 1922. Correspondence between the ranch and Victoria continued to show low beef prices with prime steers selling at .04 cents and cows at .03 per pound.

Lincoln after his return as manager.

The spring of 1924 brought additional problems for the Cariboo. Lincoln advised of a serious epidemic of smallpox in his report for March 1st 1924:

"They have a lot of smallpox through our country. Several have died. We have so far escaped. I got vaccine from Vancouver and vaccinated myself and all the help. When anyone comes here I hold him up outside until explanationis finished, L. Hannon"

One month later:

"…. We think we have the smallpox about whipt out. There was about 20 croaked including Indians. Hannon".

By July 1925 Harry Marriott was a husband and father and had his own small homestead on Big Bar Lake. But Lincoln was now 59 years old and looking for help in running the ranch. In "Cariboo Cowboy" Harry wrote:

"Towards October of 1925 I had a pretty good offer from the B.C. Cattle Co. at Canoe Creek Ranch where I had been foreman for six months in 1919. Peg and I did a lot of meditating – I was to be the foreman and have charge of the ranch work, and Peg was to look after the big ranch house and attend to the store which had all indian customers-

mostly from the reserve at Canoe Creek. We accepted this offer and I sold my little bunch of cattle and rented my little meadow to a local man called Philip Boston...."

The Marriotts, Harry, Peg and Ronnie.

Never lacking in self esteem, Harry wrote:

> *"I fell into the normal swing of the Canoe Creek Ranch at once and looked after all the practical details of the outfit under Mr. Hannon's orders – I had a very busy job. A ranch that size called for a very steady diet of everyday work, long hours, and many Sundays included, but it was something I liked doing, and the cow work just suited me to a queen's taste, because in those days I was rated as a good man around cattle...."*.

The children of the reserve had compulsory attendance at St. Joseph's Mission but no school was available locally for the non natives. As Peggy was a qualified teacher and Beaunie of school age, the additional duty of teaching was added to her chores.

Hannon had purchased a large retirement home at Robert's Creek on the Sunshine Coast and according to Harry would go down with the family for the winter. The Marriotts stayed on at Canoe Creek until the fall of 1927.

As no school was available at Canoe Creek, Emma sent two of her children south to the Big Bar Creek School. Back left is Isabelle Vedan and her brother Jimmy (with hat) in front. They were probably staying with Emma's brother Billy Grinder, as his place was about two miles west of the school.. The teacher was Miss Bessie Potts. C-1913.

Some of the sawmill's lumber for a new corral.

The Hannon home at Robert's Creek, B.C.

Above: Lincoln & Beaunie at
Canoe Creek.
Right: Beaunie at the Canoe
Creek store.
C-1925.

1927 and change was in the wind for the ranch and personnel. November 19th 1927 Lincoln received a letter from the secretary in Victoria outlining possible changes:

"We are negotiating the sale of the Company's property with Mr. Koster and Mrs. Kenworthy, and a deposit has been paid and the transaction will be completed within ten days from date unless there is some hitch in our titles. Any cattle sold in this period will be for the account of the purchaser.

If the deal goes through the company will give you a bonus of $1000.00(One thousand dollars) and I suppose the purchasers will want immediate possession so please bear this in mind and do not take on any avoidable expenses in the meantime. We will let you know definitely as soon as our titles have been accepted."

Confirmation of the deal was received by wire Dec 7th:

"Transaction with Koster concluded permit his men to have access over the range as property and cattle are now under his control but remain on the premises until you hear from Koster, keep men enough to keep things in order until Koster takes possession which will be within a week....."

Reginald Genn, secretary for the B.C. Cattle Co. and Mrs. Kenworthy (Sidney Ann Jane) and Henry Koster of the Empire Crows Bar Ranch signed the papers. The deal was very straightforward; total price of $85,000.00 with $50,000.00 cash and the balance as mortgage at 6% payable on December 6th 1932.

This was the conclusion of the pre - Koster era on the Canoe Creek Ranch. The Marriotts had left for their own ranching and resort futures, Lincoln and Emma, for full retirement at Robert's Creek.

Lincoln Hannon passed away on August 26th, 1935. His obituary, written by James Nathaniel Jerome Brown (In photo page 19) lays to rest any question of his reputation. Brown was a well-respected poet historian and long time Cariboo resident:

"Mr. L.C. Hannon, who died at Robert's Creek, was a familiar face often encountered on the cattle ranges of British Columbia. He was a type of the old class of cowboys; very skill-full in the art of handling a rope, and meritorious in all his life career.

He possessed a kindly heart to each and every individual who came under his command. He treated the Indian cowboys with the same respect as the whites. No wonder the cowboys looked upon him with a fatherly respect. He came to British Columbia in 1906, being employed by the B.C. Cattle Co. This company owned large areas of cattle ranches in different parts of the province.

In 1908 he was appointed manager of the company's cattle ranch at Canoe Creek, and this position he held until his retirement in 1928. In that year he came to Robert's Creek and purchased some land, and built a magnificent house, where he devoted himself to gardening.

I too, who have followed the cattle trail in my adolescent years, may dolefully say as it will also come to me – never again will the wild range see his cowboy form – never again shall the driven steer hear the master's voice on the overland trail – never again shall the untamed steed feel the cowboys hand. Hang the saddle up, tie the lariat on, the rider's day is past and done. God speed you well, o'er the narrow trail that all must go. So 'neath the green surf sod, at Robert's Creek, the cowboy lies low...."

J.N.J. Brown

Canoe Creek Ranch c-1927.

Before the Canoe Creek purchase the Kosters and the Kenworthys had been business partners for three years. They joined forces, the Crows Bar Ranch with the Empire Valley Ranch as equal partners in 1924. With Henry's experience in the cattle trade and available financing from the Kenworthys, the merger was to become most beneficial to both parties. The Kosters and Kenworthys had been neighbours across the Fraser River since 1915. Henry had previous dealings with Mrs. Kenworthy's relatives in Alkali Lake, when he sold his share of the partnership with H.O. Bowe to the C.E. Wynn Johnsons.

Henry's father, John Nicolas Koster, like most other early settlers, formed a family relationship with a local girl. Lucie Asteronae, a native from Alkali Lake, and John had two children, Annie born in December 1874 and Henri, born on January 22nd 1877.

Henry's father John, the Koster patriarch, was born in Luxembourg in 1828. He arrived in British Columbia in 1859 at the peak of the Fraser River gold rush amongst the crowd searching for gold. Eventually, John retired to New Westminster and passed away January 21, 1912 at St. Paul's Hospital. When Henry attended his father's death he listed John's occupation as "miner".

Henry spent his youth, from age 11, living with Mr. and Mrs. Joe Smith of the Clinton Hotel, who were mother and father to him for the next nine years. It was here that he got his education and his start in life. Leaving in 1898 with a stake of $500.00 as a well-earned bonus, he headed north to adventure.

In the early 1930's Henry gave an interview to Louis LeBourdais, a Cariboo historian, of Quesnel:

"I was born at Alkali Lake in 1877. Went to school in Clinton where I stayed and worked until 20.

Then went to Bullion, on the south fork of the Quesnelle River, where my father in association with the late John Barker, after whom Barkerville was named, and other old timers after forming a mining company among themselves, undertook to develop what they termed the South Fork Mining Company. Their development had progressed and they had completed their ditch to Pollys Lake and they had water on the ground when the late John B. Hobson appeared on the scene and bought them out, together with others, and formed the whole into what then became known as the Consolidated Cariboo Hydraulic Mining Company. Afterwards known as Bullion. Here I stayed for two years in Hobson's employ.

From there I went to the Yukon with the late Axel Gustaveson in charge of cattle for him, and where I prospected, mined and worked. From the Yukon I went to Old Mexico to see for myself what was then admitted to be the greatest cattle breeding ground in the world. It was the season when stocker cattle were being moved North into the States in thousands, some by rail and some by trail and then to be entrained and sent up into the north western States and Canada each year to the extent of hundreds of thousands of head and there ranged until they matured for market. I travelled with a trainload of them then being sent North up to Colorado then to go into feed lots and fattened on beet pulp and alfalfa. From there I travelled with a trainload of cattle to Kansas City. At which place I met up with the world famous corn fed steer in thousands. From there I went on to give the Chicago International Livestock Show, then being held, the once over. And incidentally took a flyer or two in the wheat pit as experience-with the inevitable result. I finally connected up with Pat Burns and Company in Alberta, where I worked in the yards, in the packing plant, in the saddle. One day an acquaintance appeared on the scene as cattle buyer for the Pacific Cold Storage Company of Tacoma. And which company also had a large modern plant in Dawson City as well as other points in Alaska; together with refrigerator steamers from Puget Sound to St. Michael at the mouth of the Yukon and refrigerator river steamers to Dawson City...."

Henry's friend showed up one day "stewed" and unable to perform his duties properly. Unfortunately for him the boss was up from Tacoma and sent him home, giving his job to Henry.

"....With that I got Hart's job, and which I held for some years. In 1905 I severed connections with the Company and parted from some of the finest men that it's ever been my good fortune to be associated with. It was then that I became associated with the late

H.O. Bowe at Alkali Lake by buying half interest in his ranch there and taking over the management of the property; and which we operated under the firm name of Bowe and Koster until we sold the property to Mr. C.E. Wynn Johnson and Miss S.A.J. Twigge, now widow of the late Lieu't John Kenworthy of Empire Valley. Mrs. Kenworthy and her young son now live in England but still retains her ranching interests by way of a partnership with me in all the ranching property that we now control."

After the sale of his interest in the Alkali Lake property, Henry tried his hand in the Vancouver real estate market.

By September 1911 Henry, in partnership with George S. Kerr, was operating out of the Cotton Building as a real estate and farmland broker. Real estate was in the doldrums. However, on the positive side he met and married his life long partner, 25 year old Evelyn Edith Hurst, she having arrived from England in 1911.

Evelyn and Henry Koster

The Coldwells of Jesmond with Henry and Evelyn at right.

Deciding it was time to settle down, Henry returned to the Cariboo, and with the aid of Joseph Smith of Clinton as a partner, purchased the Tom Derby Crows Bar Ranch in 1913. It was from here that the Kenworthy- Koster partnership germinated.

Louis LeBourdais, in his interview notes of 1931, documented this period;

"The interesting point here is that at a time when the cattle industry was under a serious cloud following on years of disaster, with many in the business already having gone broke, with thousands of others tottering, and while many of those who had been fortunate enough to come through with whole skins were furling up sails and resigning themselves to a spell of marking time Henry Koster, after first being hit by the slump in the price of real estate in Vancouver, then again hit in the slump in cattle prices in the years 1920/21/22/23, made his first importation of several hundred head of young stocker cattle from Alberta; in order to replace cattle that he had thrown overboard regardless

during the critical years to stave off disaster and keep going; and to follow those up with others in the years 1925/26/27 from Alberta and B.C., in herds of hundreds of head until in the aggregate they totaled thousands. During this time publicity unsolicited was withheld, and thus many incidents of interest went unrecorded. Until 1927 when late in the fall of the year with the purchase of the old established Canoe Creek Ranch, of some 18,000 acres of deeded land and some 1200 head of cattle from the B.C. Cattle Company of Victoria the outside world began to sit up and take notice. With the recent purchase of the Bishop properties in Empire Valley amounting to some 7500 acres of deeded land an unauthorized article appeared in the press crediting Koster & Kenworthy with 47,000 acres of deeded land and as being the second largest land owners in B.C. This Mr. Koster disclaims; although he explains that while the acreage with which they are credited is conservative, yet their acreage doesn't reach the 52,000 acres of deeded land as claimed belonging to the Western Canadian Ranching Co., by Mr. McMorrans. But as Mr. Koster pointed out: 'Taking Mr. McMorrans' figures as accurate, the fact remains that while his holdings are scattered throughout the Kamloops, Yale, Lillooet and Cariboo districts in different ranches and where our holdings are in one block, it looks as if we now owned the second largest ranch in British Columbia. The Douglas Lake Ranch, and which property owns well over 100,000 acres of deeded land in one block, easily comes first. All of this has been accomplished by ranch funds and from ranch earnings.'

The Douglas Lake Ranch. C-1925-Vedan Photo.

Henry wrote the following note, marked as "filler", for Louis LeBourdais;

"The history of the Empire Valley has been a heated one handed down from the days of the pioneer. Among the many relics has been the gruesome skeleton of a dispute over water for irrigation purposes that has cost it fateful influence over the valley and affected alike, the Browns, Boyles, McEwens, B.C. Cattle Co., Bishops and the Kenworthys, through the recent purchase by the Koster & Kenworthy interest of the B.C. Cattle Company and the Bishop holdings the water dispute for the first time in the history of the valley now ceases to be."

On June 1st 1947, Henry's car skidded in mud just three miles south of Churn Creek Bridge. As he tried to "chain up" the exertion was too much, and he collapsed and died of a heart attack. Henry and Evelyn's three children, John (Jack), Evelyn Joel, and Henry were still at the ranch.

Henry Koster Jr., Marion Lyster (nee-Allwood), Margaret Koster, Doug Lyster & (Evelyn) Dodie Robertson.

Above: Henry Koster & Marion Allwood.
Right:: C-1911 advertisement of Henry Senior's real estate adventure.

Henry Koster   Geo. S. Kerr

KOSTER & KERR

203 Cotton Building
— Vancouver —

REAL ESTATE
FARM LANDS

Stock Ranches
Our Specialty

If you are thinking of selling your property we would be pleased to hear from you. We charge a straight 5 per cent. commission on everything we sell, on the other hand we recognize every man's right to sell his own property or sell through another agent at any time without being liable to us for commission. Improved property is what we want— no demand for naked land.

Shirley and Jack Koster

With Henry's passing the two boys, Jack and Henry, took over the operation of the ranch. Jack being the eldest, both Henry and sister Dodie felt that naturally he should be the head man. The operation of the ranch continued this way until 1953 when a division of the assets was mutually agreed on. Henry would take the Empire Valley portion and Jack the Canoe Creek Ranch with Dodie retaining a partnership in both. The B.C. Cattle Co. Ltd is still owned and operated by the Koster family.

Annie Koster, Henry's (Sr.)older sister.

Henry and Evelyn's house at the Crows Bar, originally built
by Thomas Derby.
Below: Evelyn and son Jack at Crows Bar C-1915.

**The home of Lucy Asteronae (Bilyou), the village Esk'et .
(Early post card of Alkali Lake)**

Marion Allwood and Dodie Koster

CHURN Creek Ferry Apr. 14. 04

Although often referred to as the Churn Creek, Dog Creek or Gang Ranch Ferry, it was originally designated as the Canoe Creek Ferry.

By 1891 the Western Canadian Ranching Company had tired of waiting for the B.C. Government to build a road from their headquarters on the west side of the Fraser River to connect with Dog Creek. They constructed it on their own. With the formation of the B.C. Cattle company in 1890 and with the new road, the government finally approved a ferry crossing. It was located at the mouth of St. Mary's Creek (Churn Creek). The first contract for the operation of the Canoe Creek Ferry was awarded by the Public Works Dept to Calvin Boyle of Empire Valley, $300.00 for the year. Salary for the job increased from Calvin's $300.00 a year to $900.00 for Bill Wright, the last operator.

The Boyle family, Billy, unidentified brother, Calvin (father)
Frank Sr. and Frank Jr. at Empire Valley C-1911.

Emma Vedan, Lincoln Hannon & Sadie Vedan.
The new Gang Ranch Bridge C-1912.

WILLIAM HARRISON WRIGHT

**William Harrison Wright,
telegrapher, farmer, carpenter, ferry
operator and postmaster.**

**Placida Wright
Nee-Valenzuela**

According to Harry Marriott, the ferry was still in operation on his arrival at the river in June of 1912:

"It was getting quite late when we turned down a long hill leading to the river and the Churn Creek Ferry, as it was known then. We camped overnight with a government crew who were getting out timbers from the mountain to install what is now known as the Gang Ranch Bridge across the Fraser, which was completed in the late fall of 1912.

In the morning we drove onto the ferry, which at that time was operated by an old Missourian, named Bill Wright, who was quite a character. He had been running the ferry for quite a few years."

This "Old Missourian" was William Harrison Wright, born September 26th 1850 in Howard County, Missouri.

Collins Overland telegrapher, Bill Wright (Standing-white shirt-center of photo) among some of the prominent people of Cache Creek in 1873.

Wendy Morton, Bill's great granddaughter, in her unpublished family history, wrote the following:

"Bill immigrated to Canada in 1870. He first lived in Cache Creek and worked as a telegraph operator for the Collins Overland Telegraph. The 1881 census shows that Bill and Placida Valenzuela were living together in Cache Creek, but by the early 1880's they had moved to Dog Creek where he became postmaster from 1882 until his resignation in July 1886...."

Bill farmed and worked as a carpenter in Dog Creek. He married Placida, daughter of the well known trader and packer, Raphael Valenzuela. They had four daughters, Gertrude, Elsie, Annie and Mary.

Placida Wright (nee- Valenzuela) looking very prosperous surrounded by her four daughters. Elsie, Gertrude, Mary and Florence.

"....he worked as a carpenter and then operated the Churn Creek Ferry for many years. Placida and Bill were married in 1890. In 1893 Bill became a naturalized Canadian citizen.

Father Thomas baptized Bill on April 27th 1904.

Bill and Placida lived at Churn Creek when the 1901 census was taken. It lists Bill as a farmer with three servants, Ben F. Gibboney from the U.S. age 42 and single, Ah Lip, age 21, single from China and Kim Yow from China aged 42 and married....

....In the 1911 census he is listed as a government ferry worker, born in the U.S. and of Irish decent. Their home was listed as the Dog Creek ferry residence. Charles Morrow, an American, was boarding with them and was also listed as a government ferry worker.

Bill's wages were $900.00 per year and he worked 111 hours per week."

....In 1913 Bill had a terrible accident and froze his feet very badly, because of this he lost his right leg just below his knee. The hospital where he was operated on and recuperated at is unknown, although it may have been Ashcroft or the Royal Inland Hospital in Kamloops. After his full recovery, Bill continued his ferryman vocation. Moving north he operated the Soda Creek Ferry.

Bill Wright after his operation for frostbite.

Another of Bill recovering from his amputation at the hospital.

C-1913

Bill was a strong man and a real character and people who knew him seemed to like his eccentric ways. A true tobacco chewing Cariboo pioneer!"

As there were no male heirs, this was the end of the "Wright" name. The daughters all married; Annie to Peter Colin, Elsie to Tom Patton, Mary to Grover Hance and Gertrude to Bob French.

A contentious issue at the time and ever since, was Bill's July 8th 1893 application for a pre-emption on lot #323. Known as U.S. Meadows, the lot was finally crown granted as "Wright's Meadow" in June 1899. Today the lot has been flooded by a dam at Place lake for irrigation purposes and no longer exists. Bill spent his final years at Gustafson Lake where he passed away July 12th 1925. He was interred at the Dog Creek Cemetery.

Pierre Colin

One of the original first five settlers in Dog Creek to apply for a pre-emption was Pierre Colin, packer and trader. His great great granddaughter, Wendy Morton, has done extensive genealogy work and has supplied the following;

A very old tin type photo of Pierre Colin. Born in France in 1828, Pierre's only surviving son Peter, was born in 1868, Pierre was 40 years old. C 1858-60

"Pierre Colin"

Fr. Paimpont, Plillau illi et Vilaine, France

Pierre came to Canada and worked as a freighter/packer probably for the Hudson's Bay Company. In the 1860's he arrived in Dog Creek where he married (probably a country wife- not registered)) a Bonaparte (or possibly from Victoria) native girl, named Catherine (Karnnatkwa).

Catherine and Pierre had three sons, Peter, Joseph, and Louis. Both Joseph and Louis died in infancy.

Pierre applied for an early pre-emption and started ranching. His ranch was west of the wagon road and Oppenheimer's Hotel (It became lot # 6, group 6, Lillooet District). In 1861 Pierre and a group of men from Dog Creek applied for, and received, a water license for domestic and irrigation use. Joseph Place purchased his ranch in the mid 1880's.

Pierre kept a journal of accounts for his freight business, he hauled freight to people in Clinton, Lillooet, Soda Creek and Williams Creek. In his journal he wrote in either dollar amounts owed to him or the pounds the freight weighted. From some of the pages I surmise he must have sold merchandise to individuals. His journal is written in French and is very hard to read.

Pierre and son Peter. C 1869.

In the early 1880's Pierre Colin, Jose Tresierra and S.C. Leander Brown worked hauling freight for the Onderdonck construction camps. Andrew Onderdonck was awarded four contracts for the CPR line in 1880. He was paying $10 a ton for a few miles haulage. This was a busy time on the old corduroy road, an engineering feat built in the 1860's for the gold rush in the Cariboo. There were tons of timbers, camp supplies, explosives to be hauled for Onderdonck, also the steady flow of workers, stage coaches and wagon loads of immigrants with all their worldly goods. Pierre bought land at Big

Lake (Gustafson) where he built a house and barn. The ranch was known as the "Lower Place". Pierre died in the late 1880's and Peter Colin, his sole surviving son inherited Pierre's estate."

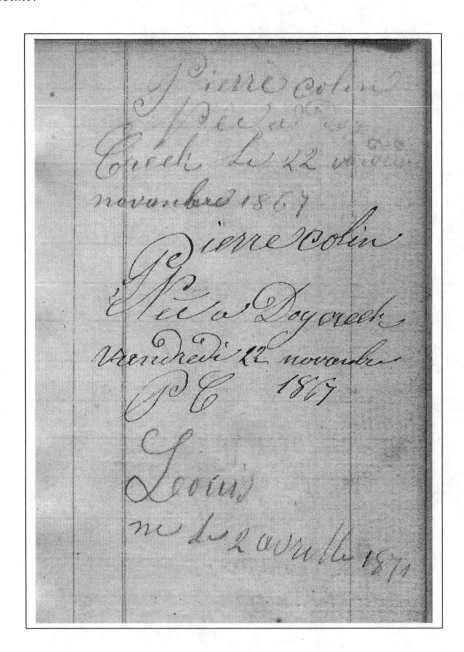

Sample page from Pierre's account book.

Peter Colin, married Bill and Placida Wright's daughter, Annie. Their wedding took place at the church of St. Paul, Canoe Creek, December 24th 1910.

Antoine Allen

Antoine Allen is a member of the B.C. Cowboy Hall of Fame. He was born in Oregon in 1853. He made his way to the Cariboo when he was just 9 years old and stayed to work for Jerome and Thaddeus Harper at their ranch on the Fraser River near Dog Creek. He drove cattle on some of the longest known trails from Washington and Oregon to the Cariboo. Antoine and Jerome Harper drove cattle to the Barkerville market at the height of the gold rush. In later years he went on beef drives with the Pat Burns Company. In 1871 at age 18, Antoine went to school in Cache Creek. Three years later he visited Oregon to reunite with his family.

B.C. Cowboy Hall of Fame member, Antoine Allen, 1936.

In an article published in the British Columbia Historical Quarterly by F.W. Laing, the author wrote about the 1876 cattle drive to Salt Lake city:

"Of the cowboys on that trip only one is alive at the present time, a Jimmy Joseph, an aged Indian living at O'Keefe Ranch near Vernon, from whom the foregoing particulars were secured…. Jimmy Joseph recalls that those engaged on the drive, in addition to Thaddeus Harper, were Antoine Allen, Charlie Connor, Tom Moore, Joe Tennice, Louis Eneas, Jimmy Rendell (a boy) a man named King and possibly one other. They provided their own horses and were paid $60.00 per month, with board and feed…."

On his return to B.C., Antoine worked at the Harper Ranch east of Kamloops. He had many wild adventures on the cattle drive trails but in time settled in the Kamloops area and married Sarah Ignace. The couple had four daughters.

On his wedding certificate, in 1963 when he was 80 years old, Alec Kalalest listed his mother as – Angelique and father as – Antoine Allen.

Antoine worked for Pat Burns on Newman Range and in later years spent his summers prospecting at the mouth of Jamison Creek on the North Thompson. Antoine Allen passed away in 1936. He was 83. Allen is buried on the Kamloops Indian Reserve.

Antoine Allen.

The Game of Lahal

Wikipedia, the internet on-line encyclopedia has the following description;

Slahal (**Lahal**) is the <u>Indigenous peoples of the Pacific Northwest Coast</u> gambling game known as stickgame, bonegame, bloodless war game, handgame, or a name specific to each language. It is played throughout the western United States and Canada by indigenous peoples. The name of the game is a <u>Chinook Jargon</u> word. The name bone game comes from the fact that the bone sets historically used were the shin bones from the foreleg of a deer or other animal.

Mary's caption " A lehal game "
Canoe Creek

The game is played with two opposing teams. There are two sets of "bones", and two sets of sticks (10 sticks per team during aboriginal times, but in modern times usually played with 5 sticks per team) and a "kick" or "king" stick -- an extra stick won by the team who gets to start the game (in some areas a kick stick is not used). When a game is in play, one of the two teams will have two sets of "bones", shown above. When your team is guessing, your objective is to get the right bone, the one without the stripe. When you have the bones, your objective is to make sure the other team guesses wrong on the bones set. When the other team guesses wrong, you gain a point. When a team has the two sets of bones, two separate individuals will hide the bones and swap them around from hand to hand (each person has a striped and non-striped bone). Eventually the bones are brought forward, but are concealed as to not show the other team what one has a stripe on it. The game is usually accompanied by drumming and singing used to boost the morale of the team. The side that has the bones sings, while the other tries to guess. The musical accompaniment is also sometimes used to taunt the other team. Gambling could be done by players, or spectators of a match, placing bets on teams, or individual matches within the game between one guess and the other team's bone hiders.

Oral histories indicate that slahal is an ancient game, dating to before the last ice age. In the Coast Salish tradition, the Creator gave stickgame to humanity as an alternative to war at the beginning of time. Thus the game straddles multiple roles in Native culture -- it is at once entertainment, a family pastime, a sacred ritual and a means of economic gain (through gambling). These juxtapositions are sometimes difficult to comprehend for the Western mind, but to many members of the Native community they are woven together effortlessly as a harmonic whole.

A game of "Stick".

Photo Gallery

The above photo was in Mary Palmantier's album and the caption was "Our people as they dressed around 1900".

Taken in 1937 at the Green Lake Stampede. Back row – Cecilia Tenale, Eliza Tinmusket, Toddie Prydatok, Pauline Alexander. Children - Nancy and Augustine Tenale.

Back row – Unidentified
Front – Eliza and Louie
Tinmusket.

Louie Tinmusket and
Christopher, Canim Lake Chief.

Louie Tinmusket at the Gang Ranch.
Photo was taken by Fred Boyle of Empire Valley.

Madeline Seymour

Louie and Alec Seymour.

Augustine Seymour
At the Canoe Creek store.

**Left-Tony Sampson & Alex Kalalest.
Above-Basil, Angus & Alex Seymour.**

**Noel Tenale's house, Celestine Camille (seated)
Rita Tenale (right).**

Left: Harry Dick Johnson
Right: "Buckskin" Louie Camille

Maudie and Victor Lewis.

**Paying last respects
at Canoe Creek.**

Mary Palmantier's caption for these photos is "The people took hunters out to the game".

Joe Edwards with new
"Woolies" at the Canoe
Creek store.
Joe, known as "Camp"
(A happy fellow)

Louis Seymour
and Joe Sargent
at the Canoe
Creek House.
Note: photo was
taken before
Louis' accident
with his left eye.

Cecilia Tenale &
Irene Archie

Francis Sampson & ?.

Seraphine Camille (left) & ?

Above: Dick Jime (Jimmy).
Right: Lucy Billy and Geoff Place.

Unknown, Basil Seymour, Johnny and Jack Duncan

Above: Johnny Duncan
Right: Cecilia Tenale
Below: Celine Johnson
Below Right: Mary Tenale

Back: Rosalie Rosette, Sarah Bill, Elizabeth, the rest unidentified.

Kenuckwux & Charlie Sampson.

George, Alfred & Doris Sargent.

Above: Alex Seymour
Below: Lucy Sampson and
Elizabeth Sampson

Above: Andrew Meshue
Below:Madeline Duncan

Above: Sarah Camille.

Right: Jack Duncan.

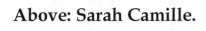

Charlie Sampson, Sarah Bill, Willy Billy & Rosalie Rosette.

Nellie, Emma and Jimmy Vedan feeding Canada Geese at the B.C.
Cattle Co. equipment shed.

Jimmy practicing for "Buffalo Bill's" Wild West Show, like his uncle
James Grinder.

**Top left: Sadie Vedan
Top Right: Susan Billy and
Patsy Billy holding babies.**

Right: Pharita Tenale

**Vivian Sampson, David Sampson, Dave Sampson, Ralph Bill,
Thomas Sampson, Willard Seymour.**

**Mary Jane Billy & Willard
Seymour.**

Jason Peter Sampson

Left: Joe Rosette
Below: Nelson Chelsea
(from Esket, B.C.)

Julia George, Charlie and Maude Spahan. (from Esket B.C.)

**Top Left: Lena Johnson
Above: Alice Belleau
and Old Charlie
Antoine.
Left:
Jack Long with two
unidentified children.
Esket, B.C.**

Frank Bones

Maude Spahan & Julia George.

The Squinahan sisters, Delyia and Lily.
Esket, B.C.

Left: Tom Johnson
Above: Augusta Sampson, Matilda Grinder and Laura Harry.

Julia Dick, Arthur Rosette (Wahoo) and Theresa Paul.

Above: Standing: Alec Rosette, Arthur Rosette, & Dorothy Johnson Dick.
Seated: Jimmy Corn, Norman Dick and William Rosette.
Below: Pete Bones.

Left:
Fred Louie, unidentified hunter and Augustine Rosette.

Right: Nora and Annie Rosette.
Below: Chris and Fred Louie at the Gang Ranch.

Left: Peter Colin.
Below: Placida Wright- Pigeon (nee Valenzuela) & daughter Florence.

Below:
Miss Good , Mary and Grover Hance at the Hance ranch.

Right:
Gertrude and
Placida Wright.

Below: Peter Colin
and Grover Hance.

Right: Three of the Wright
girls, Florence (Florie), Mary
and Elsie.

Left: Peter Colin, Mr. Krebs and Marc Pigeon.
Below: Elsie (nee Wright) and Tom Patton October 2nd 1915 @ Springhouse.

Mary Hance (nee Wright) with husband Grover to her right.
The outside cowboys were Grover's brothers.

Left:
Ione Colin, Grover Hance and
Tommy Patton.

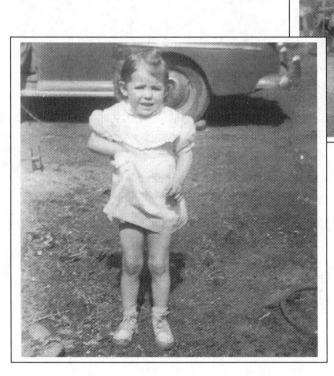

Above: Hazel Colin, granddaughter
of Placida and Bill Wright.

Left:
Wendy Morton, great granddaughter
of Placida and Bill Wright.

Right: Rosalie Sargent and
Rosie Seymour.
Below: Angeline Rosette,
Julia Louie, Fred Louie,
Pete Bones and
unidentified hunter.

Pascal Adams,
Basil, Louie &
Jimmy Seymour,
and Dora Billy in
front.

Ralph Bill

Louie Seymour & Antoine Billy

Sheila and
Selina Kalalest

Louie Johnson (right)

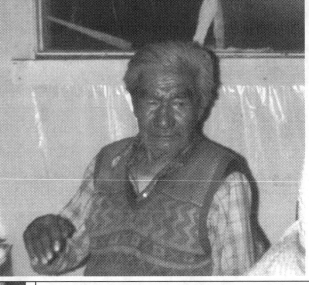

Edward (Stobie) Billy

100 Years Old

**Stobie's
sister,
Lena Jack**

Unidentified from the Canoe Creek area. Who are they?

Three more
unidentified

THE VISION IN THE WOODS

The noon hush of October was as sweet
As passage of South-wending birds was fleet.
In Autumn's peaceful lights I scanned afar
Scenes soon to be eclipsed by Winter's scar.

The distant woods were laden, crimson, gold,
A mass of beauty, gay above dark mould;
And so has Life its contrasts, happy, sad,
Where tears and laughter mingle, good and bad.

I watched the languid chain of shadows pass,
Imposed by clouds upon a sea of glass,
And with calm folded thoughts serenely stood
Where sunrays warmly gleamed through frost-nipped wood.

The gray leaves fell, their hour being past,
Wild flowers, roses, drooped and fell at last;
Summer was gone with all her gray-garbed train,
Now, brilliant colors would be changed to plain.

That nature has her rules for all is clear:
No more than flowers should we her changes fear,
For us each season has its fitting hue,
And we, like flowers, fade, then bloom anew.

James Nathaniel Jerome Brown

CONTRIBUTORS

Kathy Paulos

Audrey Higbee

Beaunte Mumford

John Schreiber

Mike Hocevar

Karen Logan

Mildred Kalalest

Nancy Carrillo

Wendy Morton

Shirley Robbins

Darlene
Louie

Victorine
Alphonse

Jeannie & Mark
Cawston

Josephine
Holt

Betz
Ratch

Rosalie
Sargent

Augustine
Tenale

Flora
Tenale

Ida Duncan

Selina &
Warren
Koster

Earl Cahill

Bill Sworts

INDEX

Bibliography

Victims of Benevolence-Elizabeth Furniss

Looking Back at the Cariboo-Chilcotin-Irene Stangoe-Heritage House publishing.

They call it the Cariboo-Robert Skelton-Sono Nis Press

Shushwap, Volume 2-James Teit

Ashcroft Journal

Williams Lake Tribune

The British Colonist

Cariboo Cowboy-Harry Marriott-Gray Publishing

The Lovell Chronicle-June 28th 2007

Wikipedia-Game of Slahal

Esketemc First Nation-Wright's pre-emption inquiry (Indian Claims
	Commission)

Some Pioneers of the Cattle Industry-F.W. Laing

B.C. Cowboy Hall of Fame archives

Ka-mi-akin- The Last Hero of the Yakimas-A.J. Splawn

Printed in the United States
By Bookmasters